THE

SEEDS

THE SEEDS

POEMS

CECILY PARKS

ALICE JAMES BOOKS

NEW GLOUCESTER, MAINE · ALICEJAMESBOOKS.ORG

10 9 8 7 6 5 4 3 2 1

Alice James Books are published by Alice James Poetry Cooperative, Inc.

Alice James Books
Auburn Hall
60 Pineland Drive, Suite 206
New Gloucester, ME 04260
www.alicejamesbooks.org

Library of Congress Cataloging-in-Publication Data

Names: Parks, Cecily, author.
Title: The seeds : poems / by Cecily Parks.
Other titles: Seeds (Compilation)
Description: New Gloucester, Maine : Alice James Books, 2025.
Identifiers: LCCN 2025006591 (print) | LCCN 2025006592 (ebook) | ISBN
9781949944891 (trade paperback) | ISBN 9781949944495 (epub)
Subjects: LCGFT: Poetry.
Classification: LCC PS3616.A7554 S44 2025 (print) | LCC PS3616.A7554
(ebook) | DDC 811/.6--dc23/eng/20250404
LC record available at https://lccn.loc.gov/2025006591
LC ebook record available at https://lccn.loc.gov/2025006592

Alice James Books gratefully acknowledges support from individual donors, private foundations, the National
Endowment for the Arts, and the Poetry Foundation (https://www.poetryfoundation.org).

Cover art: Leila Kempner, "Mexican Buckeye," 2023

Table of Contents

FOR CALLA AND JUNE

And no backyard is ever overrated

—BERNADETTE MAYER

GIRLHOOD

was when I slept in the woods
bareheaded beneath jagged
stars and the membranous
near-misses of bats, when
I first tasted watercress,
wild carrot, and sorrel,
when I was known
by the lilac I hid beside,
and when that lilac, burdened
by my expectations of lilacs,
began a journey
without me, as when
the dirt road sang, *O,*
rugosa rose, farewell,
and ran behind the clipped
white pine hedge into
the immeasurable
heartbreaks of the field.

ONE

HUNDRED-YEAR-OLD WINDOW

I wanted the hundred-year-old window
to open, as I assumed it had for many people
before I lived in this house and thought

to put a desk beside it. It was stuck.
Its watery glass gave onto hackberry branches
and thick black power lines and, by way of its delicate blur

of the scene, made the eyes turn and
return to it, like a woman everyone
looks at, as if, looked at long enough, she might

be seen through and therefore invisible.
The window did not grant me the permission
I thought a window, no matter how antique,

owed me, which was the permission to have
hackberry-cooled air drift across my desk while I write
the word *hackberry*, a name I learned after a storm

splintered one of the tree's limbs and I called
an arborist to saw it off. Because of its crowded
easily broken branches, the hackberry is trash,

the arborist told me, and offered to remove it
altogether, even though it cooled the house
and, as I later read, is one of the first trees to grow

on scarred earth. When I called the carpenter
to fix the window, I learned that it was operated
by pulleys and ropes with cooperating cylindrical weights

hidden in the wood frame on each side
of the sash. It seemed cruel and just
that even when I learned how the window worked

its workings still denied me sight of them,
and when I learned about the hackberry
it was an invitation to destroy the tree.

You'll say I only pay attention to things
when they're broken and I'll say, *Too late*.
At sunset the window can look like water

a wounded animal has walked through.
Some days I'm the animal, some days I wound it.

HARVEST

The grackles plummet down to pierce the lawn

for seeds and fat brown live oak acorns

and ignore the orange plastic watering cans

my daughters drop in the cold grass, my daughters

saying, *Goodnight grass*, as if the blades they'd watered

by hand were their daughters, as if the grass

were a feeling they'd been feeling, greenly

reckoning the evening, the ball moss falling from the trees,

the sun circling the crouched shade of the weeping

persimmon tree as mildly as the knife rounds

the persimmon I bring inside so I can say

of the pierced skin, *Look, this is the color we*

want sunset to be, the color of the plastic

watering cans shocking the dark that falls

over the suggestions of footprints in the grass,

the oily grackles, and the acorns battering

our metal roof while I feed my ravenous daughters

a soft dinner that they clutch with grubby hands and gnaw.

EPIPHYTE INTERLUDE

When ball
moss falls
we feel
most at
a loss
to explain
why this
soft bomb
of sticks
and fine
jade colored
fronds loud
with naught
drops to
us: does
the tree
let the
moss go
or does
the tree
ask us
to hold
the moss?

DATURA

When evening came at the end of a day
that I'd consumed by saying brutal things
to the people I love most,
I fled our home into a night whose heat
so closely approximated my own
that it was as if my body had no end:
I was the dark that lay under all
the live oaks and coalesced at each spine
of the neighborhood cactuses I'd learned
to call prickly pear. If my sweat
poured down the hill to fill the dry creek bed,
I couldn't see it by the light of the six
mercury vapor lamps that pretended,
from a moontower, to be the moon.
Only when a flower spilled its cool white
light onto the hot road that had become
part of my feet did I finally stop
running. I wanted that flower.
I wanted it in my garden so that each night
I'd have an object to hold
my gaze while I counted my cruelties
and my daughters slept and my husband washed
our wood floors of the crumbs and grease
that lured roaches indoors.
Should I have known love
would make me vicious toward the people
I loved, that every gorgeous part
of the night-blooming beauty plant I craved

was poison? I learned later to call it
jimsonweed, moonflower, or datura.
But alone that night I believed I might
be buried alive with that plant because
of how it absolved my viciousness with light.
I was like the owl who believes the moon
streaks mice with silver
just for her. I was a new wife and a new
mother. I was in the dirt that grew the flower.

A PRIVATE WELL

Up the pre-dawn hill I ran
on roads that had been dirt
until the decade of my birth.
The hilltop's white house
had a lawn so lush
it was enviable, or so I thought,
until a sign told me
it was watered by a private well.
The private well
was the enviable thing
then, for this was a drought
year. I paid for water,
knew that I could choose not
to water my lawn and chose
to water my lawn.
I had a private well
of shame for wanting green
when weather sent dust.
As I ran uphill in the dark,
I called everyone who'd ever hurt
the earth a motherfucker, but in
a whisper, so as not to wake
the neighborhood, so you
could be forgiven
for thinking I was saying it
to myself. I could barely breathe.
To run uphill more efficiently,
I'd been told to imagine someone

attacking me from behind
and use my elbows to fight
them off. I suffered inadequately.
I could see I was in a neighborhood
with expensive homes
for sale when sunrise set fire
to the city.

ON FIRE

It's May and I've never seen the firewheels so thick by the side of Interstate 35. There were five continuous years of drought in this part of Texas, but today the burn bans are all in counties west of us. The wild flowering firewheels (*Gaillardia pulchella*) blanket the roadsides: no wonder the bees are delirious. Give them these grenadine pinwheels tipped with yellow and the guzzle is on.

It's May and the authorities are looking for the suspect: a hunter who failed to properly extinguish a warming fire and was last seen carrying a hunting rifle and a compound bow. He is believed to have ignited the fire that burned at the end of last summer for over two weeks, wiped out 55 homes, and came within a quarter mile of a place I love. I've driven west along the road that the fire almost crossed, past the cabins where cowboys slept to keep close to their cows in winters none of us remember, past the willows in the moose marshes and up into the lodgepole pines and aspen. Where the road ends, I've straddled a jangling creek and climbed though the meadow of lupine, coneflowers, oxeye daises, and lilies, carrying a stone full of my want to place on the first mountaintop I came to.

QUESTION: What is the best way to make a fire with two sticks?
ANSWER: Make sure one of the sticks is a match.

In the poem "Verses upon the Burning of our House, July 10th, 1666" Anne Bradstreet writes: "That fearful sound of 'fire' and 'fire,' / Let no man know is my Desire." My students and I discuss the ambiguity of these lines. Keep it a secret, she could be saying, I want a fire to divest me of all my earthly material burdens, these books, brooms, and aprons. Or: I never want to hear the word fire, she could be saying, never again want to see the beds of my children blasted to ash. *What you think?* I ask my students. *I think Anne Bradstreet didn't have a lot to do and was bored, so she wrote poems*, one student offers. I remind him of the seventeenth century, what we know of life in the Massachusetts Bay Colony, and the labor of pregnancy, childbirth, and caring for your eight children who survived infancy. How she found the time to write, I'll never know. People on the Internet ask: *When did Anne Bradstreet's house burn down? What is the theme of upon the burning of our house? Why did Anne Bradstreet write upon the burning of our house?* The poem answers these questions, but searchers want the Internet's answers instead.

It's May. Here, under the paloverde trees: an aftermath of yellow flowers expertly self-extricated from their branches. Each limp yellow blossom casts a miniscule shadow on the gravel and asphalt. The trees massage the flowers with shadow, but the flowers are having a conversation with the sun. I bend to the ground to catch their words. "Oh, oh, oh, I'm on fire," says one, quoting Bruce Springsteen; "You burn me," says one, quoting Sappho; "Burn me O Lord," says another, quoting John Donne. One flower—in this heat!—drapes blankets around herself and prepares to sleep.

It's May when the cheerleader marries the captain of the football team. She follows him to the oil refineries in Galveston. The refinery where he works catches fire and she's a widow at 22. She marries again, and when her second husband comes home from World War II, he works for an oil company too. A different company or the same company, does it matter? My grandparents move every year—Texas, New Mexico, Colorado, Wyoming—looking for oil. One of the towns they live in is called Tahoka, from the Comanche word for fresh water.

It's said that in May, farmers released clouds of ladybugs to protect their crops from insect pests. When it was time to burn the fields for the following year, the farmers sang variations of this rhyme to warn the ladybugs away, to keep them safe.

> Ladybird, ladybird fly away home,
> Your house is on fire and your children are gone,
> All except one,
> And her name is Ann,
> And she hid under the baking pan.

As our summers burn hotter, believe what you will; think what you want.

> Ladybird, ladybird, fly away home,
> Your house is on fire,
> Your children shall burn!

It's May and I'm reading *On the Banks of Plum Creek* to my daughters. I come to the chapter titled "Wheels of Fire." Next thing I know, big burning tumbleweeds blown by the prairie wind are setting fire to the grass, blazing towards Laura and the dugout house she, her mother, and her two sisters are taking care of while Pa is away looking for work. Ma beats the rolling fires with wet gunnysacks wound around the end of a mop; Laura and her sister keep soaking gunnysacks in the creek and filling the pail with water. Then here comes Mr. Nelson, a neighbor, running over to help protect the haystacks piled high as palace gold.

It may be that what I want doesn't matter. A UPS truck rips the lowest branch of a cedar tree and the air gets hotter. It is not without drought that the rosemary becomes a fine lace. It is not without thirst that the tangled tomato plant yields blossoms but no fruit. The grape leaves singe at their edges. I stick a cedar bough in the filler neck of our car's gas tank and another next to the fire extinguisher. The last time it rained, they found the body of a dead woman, naked, in the river.

LOQUAT

Come late spring, the branches bear

creamy blooms then pulpy orange half-sweet

three- or four-stoned fruits that slip to the dirt

that all things living leave behind, dirt

that children play in, dirt my daughters played in

back when my daughters thrilled to blink-eye dolls

and the story about a cat who marries an owl, so that when

with bare feet they mashed the loquats into the dirt

and said they were dancing along the moon, I knew

what they meant to say but not what they said:

the owl and the pussycat in their book

danced *by the light of the moon, the moon, the moon* as if

desire required clarity and did not, as my daughters did

(as desire did), confuse me. Everybody who lived

in this dry place we'd come to raved

for the loquats lolling on tongues of shade, the fruit

I was meant to want more of but wanted no more of, and not

without sadness I knew that I couldn't make myself want

more children, and that this want of naught

brought me closer to the dirt and farther from being

alive enough to look at light and see it: a candle,

a gold ring pierced through a pig's nose, a moon

swinging so close I could eat it.

GOLD RING

Life is short and I still haven't
slept with a married man, swum
in a fairy pool fringed by gorse
on the Isle of Skye, or swallowed
a gold ring. My finger
in another's mouth: been there. What key
opens the shed where I keep the spare?
A ring of petals rests on the table
because I touched the yellow flower
I suspected of being dead. All gone,
all gone like the song of the baby
who has eaten all her food. All gone,
the days when I could have been
doing my undones and been, perhaps,
undone. Oh wait, hold on, I slept
with a married man not long ago.
He was my husband. My days go on.

CLIPPING

I have not seen you in over a decade
when out of a beloved novel
falls a newspaper clipping you used as a bookmark.
Creepy, my husband says, holding up an article
about an army officer who killed his wife
and severed his own tongue to escape
interrogation. Now I know you
didn't finish the book my husband
is reading next to me in bed, now
he will always have read more of it
than you did. You were into that kind
of story, I explain to my husband, it inspired
your fictions, which you asked me to read
and edit. When the novel you never finished reading
was published, one critic wrote
that it "worships too long at the altar
of the intellect," which no one said that year
about a novel written by a man.
My husband hands me the soft scrap.
I love how history
never riles his vindictiveness.
I used to think you didn't like women.
It took me a long time to realize you didn't
like me. Forgive me, history
always riles my vindictiveness, which is why
I prefer to pretend I never worshipped
at the altar of your intellect, never
met you. Eventually, even tranquilly,

I may read the book I helped you write.

SUNDAY

So this is Sunday evening
under the live oak behind the kitchen
where the Rose of Sharon
spills purple tea onto the grass,
the yellow bells sound yellow alarms
from tall stalks, and the sunflowers peep
over the fence into the street
where car tires lap at the pavement
and walkers and joggers and dogs and strollers
pass. Our weeping persimmon
makes a small room
under its branches that children
younger than mine could inhabit
for an afternoon. Squirrels chase
each other up the live oak trunk, scratching
the bark. Crape myrtle, peach, plum:
our tiny arboretum.
We had another tree that had room
for two girls to sit in it, but the winter freeze
killed it. Gone, too,
the neighbor whose name I never learned
who yelled at speeding cars in her front yard
wearing only a long t-shirt and underwear
with her ageless legs for all to see,
especially me, from my kitchen, as I waited then,
as I wait now, for my daughters' tears
to come the way they do every Sunday evening
because we cut down their climbing tree

and tomorrow is a school day, and they don't care
about the sky dropping pink and orange curtains
around the neighbor's, ending an opera
about a house that held a woman's life
that some tomorrow will scrape down.

BACKYARD RHYME

Compost, gate post, lamppost, leaf,
possum tail and possum teeth.
Sapling, dove wing, honeybee,
three peaches on the tree.
One turned brown,
one stayed green,
one was pierced by grackle beak.
P-I-T spells pit, sings she.

TWO

DISPATCHES FROM THE ALLEY

Today I'm walking the alley behind our house, visiting the kingdom of rough shade. A mop rests against my neighbor's chain link fence, its teardrop loops of purple string drying in the heat. Wisteria, I think, because it's spring and I have flowers on the brain. Next, a bank of widows' tears, long-stemmed purple two-petaled flowers buoyed by the long grasses and alley-side bracken. I'm surprised to find stores of purple in the mop and the weeds: purple for the luxury we lace into the mundane, and purple for grief. I pass a wooden fence, some arched rebar, a cedar, a palm, and a hackberry. Then here comes a breeze, and someone's wind chimes release a fragment of song that promises neither beginning nor crescendo nor resolution.

One night not long ago, the wind chimes in our Texas mountain laurel sounded the jangling warning of an oncoming storm. In our bedroom, my husband confessed he'd never liked wind chimes, but he was trying to. He told me his former love hated wind chimes, and aligning his dislike with hers felt treacherous now that he was making a home with me. The clattering outside our window went on, as if whole sets of antique silverware were dropping out of the sky. It was not pretty. I thought but didn't say, *Okay, you love me.* That's all.

There are storms in the forecast all week, and today as I walk, I can imagine rain running down the gentle slope of the alley and making it mud. The alley widens, narrows, and widens depending on the vegetation alongside it. I walk east past the long-stemmed spreading hedge parsley whose flowers are tiny puffs of particulate white, then past the bottle partway full of red Powerade, the crushed Monster Energy can, the pink and yellow Ziplocs filled with nothing, and a mound of hacked-off green pads that once composed a prickly pear cactus. My neighbors and I give the alley so much to hold, such as the middle stripe of this unpaved road that a chassis clears, where grass grows.

The wind chimes that I hear now aren't mine. All of a sudden, the blue jays are screaming and I see why: here comes the neighborhood brown-and-white cat, walking the tightrope-like top of a metal fence between two backyards. I feel a twist of fear in my center when the cat crosses one paw in front of the other, makes eye contact with me, and doesn't stop stalking. I know this cat. This is the cat that dallyingly dismantled a mourning dove in our front yard the summer my daughters asked me if I would die. *Everybody dies only after they've lived a long and beautiful life*, I lied, as feathers gamboled in the air.

The yellow flowers on long stems are called hairy cat's ear. They tangle in the dried grasses and in the vines with heart-shaped leaves. I pass a crumpled Coke can, grasses growing through a driveway's black ornamental gravel, a purple blossom blaring out of the bindweed, and a purple ground cherry too. By the time I come to a fig tree with small green swells of figs, the alley seems so violent and extravagant that I believe the horseherb growing up around a discarded green plastic flowerpot will devour it.

At the end of the alley, a dumpster stands flush against a house that's next for demolition. Used to be, a pickup that advertised a karate school on its rear windshield parked there. Each Halloween, the family handed out Capri-Suns and bags of candy so big you had to receive them with two hands. At Christmastime, the Santas, reindeer, penguins, and polar bears on the roof and porch emitted enough light to dazzle the street. When I came to the alley, I wanted to discover that it holds up the neighborhood like a spine, or that it's a romantic passageway overarched by silky pomegranate blossoms. I wanted to figure out why, when I watched my twin daughters disappear down it on the back of my husband's cargo bike on the first day of kindergarten, and I prayed that no one would walk into their school with a gun, it was the alley I prayed to. Now I want to tell about the house that's going down, how it has decorative glass beads embedded in the lawn, and how my daughters, when they were younger, used to pry them out and pocket them, because they were jewels.

THREE

LIGHTNING RHYME

August, wind gust, rain lust, drought,
heart-shaped leaves and heart-shaped doubt.
Live oak, pin oak, hackberry,
sun-singed lace in place of rosemary.
Lightning flashes,
lightning branches,
mimicking the oak it splits in three.
Which one sings, *O woe is me?*
The oak or the electricity?

THE RIO GRANDE

This is
the summer
the Rio
Grande will
remember as
the summer
the children
were taken
from fathers
and mothers
who brought
them to
the Rio Grande
The law
of drought
has delivered
its trouble
to the
Rio Grande
where ranchers
once lived
in a
house so
low to
the thorny
windblown ground
you have
to crawl

to enter

its darkness

as I

did after

the Rio Grande

dried from

my hand

The Rio

Grande I

dipped my

hand in

after crossing

over into

motherhood is

also the

one sawing

through the

desert like

a sustained

howl After

the Rio

Grande dried

from my

hand its

disappearance accumulated

sadness when

I learned

a ribbon

of stones

would replace

the Rio

Grande threading

through green
ground-puffs of
mourning lovegrass
and cacti
with flowers
like the
beginnings of
wildfire When
it thunders
one summer
night I
am not
sure if
I am
hearing the
drought breaking
or the
watery sound
of an
endangered animal
drinking from
the Rio
Grande its
fear the
size of
a small
ammo can
The Rio
Grande holds
Texas in
the palm
of its

hand or
could it
be the
Rio Grande
is really
the fist
of the
United States
I am
not sure
the Rio
Grande remembers
turquoise-tipped dragonflies
bobbling over
the ruined
dock the
cloud-haired American
grandmothers who
ooooed over
the rapids
in a
pillowy raft
the cactus
with flowers
like pools
of blood
the time
its tributaries
met and
like lovers
pushed their
beds together

so when
the Rio
Grande turns
over in
its bed
creating the
rustle of
the Rio Grande
I ask
Which one
of the
children is
crying because
how can
anyone sleep
through this
storm

TEXAS NATIVES

Apache plume
Mexican blazing star
Blue agave
Cherokee sedge
Mexican devil-weed
Mexican elderberry
Esperanza
Fall obedient plant
Firewheel
Mexican feathergrass
Gaura
Mexican hat
Hierba del cáncer
Indian blanket
Jimsonweed
Mexican juniper
Kingcup cactus
Lluvia de oro
Mexican marigold
Mexican navelwort
Oreja de ratón
Mexican panicgrass
Queendevil
Red-spike Mexican hat
Mexican silktassel
Mexican thistle
Uña de gato
Velas de coyote

Mexican weeping juniper
Xcanchac-che
Mexican yellowshow
Zitherwood

AMISTAD GAMBUSIA

Gambusia amistadensis

To obtain the perfect idea
      of nothing, the Puritan minister Jonathan Edwards wrote,
"We must think of the same

that the sleeping rocks dream of."
      Here, lined up on my windowsill:
nine gray rocks, faceted with pale yellow

and orange, powdery to the touch
      and warm from the sun.
With equanimity, light pours through

the window onto all of them.
      If they dream of you
then I can't write about you

without writing about them, because no one else
      can play their part, glossily lining
the bottom of Goodenough Spring,

the West Texas creek where you dart
      like a shard of filigree, unblinkingly
swimming in a body

of water probably named for a family
      with an old English name originally used
for someone whose accomplishments were average.

Gambusia, your name,

        comes from the Cuban Spanish word

for nothing.

           May I call you

        Nothing. There is no hurry for you

to answer or tell me which

is sadder: the dreams of rocks

        or speaking to nothing.

The size of an ocotillo spine, you're too small

to be fished for sport, not even the way

        I'm fishing now, flipping through natural histories

for a mention of you, expecting a glint

of iridescence to swim up from an index.

        In the heat of this devastating summer,

you seem as diminutively monumental as a glass paperweight

pinning down notes about the difference

        between erasure and banishment

and, yes, I meant to write *vanishment* and now

I want both. When you appear

        in *Vanishing Fishes* and *Battle Against Extinction*

you remind me that vanishment

can be conferred, like the language

        of war, even onto a weaponless minnow

who weighs less than a bookmark.

When engineers build a dam across the Rio Grande
        connecting Mexico and the United States
and name it Amistad, the dam becomes a symbol

of friendship, but when the Rio Grande is dammed,
        water rises in Goodenough Spring, knocking
the stones shining under you,

churning and turbid and suddenly flooding
        the creek, confluence, and headspring
that sustain a single species of gambusia

no one knows about

        until 1968, post-dam, mid-flood, too late,
        when ichthyologists discover you
darting through the suddenly flooding ocotillo

and honey mesquite as the water rises
        over riverbanks.
The scholarly paper that declares your discovery

declares your endangerment, and the authors
        net and transfer you to a field laboratory
in Austin. Later, they move you to the Dexter National Fish Hatchery

in New Mexico in the 1970s and 80s
        because you have "no historic habitat
remaining in nature" and there, in tanks, you go

full ghost.

May I call you extinct?
I was the second-to-last person
to see them alive,

says the ichthyologist in the museum I visit,
          handing me a warm jar of you
jostling together in formaldehyde.

The last person to see you alive
          is dead. I put you back
in the ichthyologist's hands, he puts you back

at the back of a warehouse shelf. You are removed
          from the endangered species list
when I'm eleven, the same age

my twin daughters are now, now watching
          the ocean throw thousands
of fish onto the Texas Gulf Coast. Take them,

the ocean seems to say, and not kindly, because
          they're dead, mostly asphyxiated
Gulf menhaden silvering the sand with the last

of their dazzle.

          I once had a teacher
     who asked me, *What is another word*
for lostness? I used the word too much.

I don't remember my answer, lost now,
          a little nothing to line up on the windowsill

next to the rocks, two seed pods, a burr,

one lobe of a tiny white mussel shell
            with a buttery interior, and two vials
of water from the Amistad Reservoir

that a friend collected from your demolished habitat
            to help me think of you, a fish named
for the dam that obliterated you.

                    What did it feel like
to lose your only home
            is a question you do not have to answer.

After all, I am not your teacher.

THE BATS

They're like little brown handkerchiefs waving goodbye
in the sky. Goodbye oaks, dogwoods, ashes and elms.
Goodbye, caves. Goodbye, mines and the coal
that lit up the night. Goodbye, night that the bats fly by.

The bats fly by twilight, or bat-light, and their bat-flight is full
of waltz and veer and feeding in midair. Goodbye,
arcane glide over the woodlot. Goodbye, tiny pink tongue
that drinks on the wing from the pond with the apricot glow.

The apricot glow fills the carriage window of the overnight train
rushing two fields away and then (Goodbye!) it's too late
to ask who's inside or what they're saying. The bats
hear sumac, nettle, and wild grape when a woman hears nothing.

A woman hears that elves wear bat-fur coats, or witches
cook with wool of bat, and goodbye, Dunsinane. *Goodbye,*
the old wives say, believing that when a bat flies into a woman's hair,
she hears voices that remain indefinite and goes insane.

Voices that remain indefinite reverberate through the cloister
of hickories and bounce off the goldenrod and poison ivy. They
compose the stream, the fall-flowering anemones, and the mosquito's
wing, indexing the distance between the hawthorn and extinction.

Because the tincture of night is darkened by their goodbyes:
My umbrella was cut in half, says one. *Goodbye, havens
and hibernacula,* says another. *I never knew a belfry,* says one.

I spent my whole life shouting hello, says another.

Sleep with me, the bats sing each winter before hibernation.
Sleep with me, sings the baby bat to its mother in the roost
in the bark of the decaying maple tree. *Sleep with me*,
the maple sings, past the season of green twisting keys.

DECIDUOUS INTERLUDE

The morning
bends down
to meet
the canopy
that we
walk under.
We know
the moss,
forget-me-nots, and
blue-green spruce
but we
want to
be known
by the
woods. We
say without
saying, *Forget
me not.*
We listen
to maples,
ash, and
oaks without
hearing, but
not hearing
doesn't mean
that we
aren't spoken
to. What

was that?
Leaves rustle
as if
to say,
You forget.
We forgot.

BOUGAINVILLEA

Someone cut the wayward stick
of bougainvillea that burst out
from between the slats of our fence

into the sidewalk air. It had blossoms
and it had thorns, tiny disquisitions
on the freedom of beauty. The someone

who cut the stick must walk
with shears in their pocket, and the shears
must dig at the pocket's interior

so that the fabric at bottom
is almost a hole holding the blades
in a metal beak. I could see

how the person who cut the bougainvillea
may have been a woman
who knew that the pursuit of beauty was outwardness

with no object, no point
of rest. She herself may have been beautiful
or may have been beautiful

once, as they say when they want
to say something about an older woman.
The thorns may have raked

her calves one too many times.
Her dog may have wanted too much
to unbutton the flowers' blouses

with his wet nose. She cut the stick
just at the gap in the fence slats where it leapt
into the faithless air, hanging there its ladder

of magenta fire, a memory of when
two people first undressed
in a foreign country, a library of desire

left for me to find and throw into the street, down
a storm drain, or into a shapely vase.
The shearswoman may have been tired of being made

to look with eyes disciplined
by beauty but could not cut out her eyes, could not
not see the sidewalk, a smudged chalk drawing

someone's child made, and the smears
her plastic-bagged gathering of dogshit
inevitably left behind under

the bougainvillea. She imagined a field rank
with grasses, goldenrod, and ferns, and herself
inside it, inside a tractor cab inside it,

and on the back of the tractor was hitched
a flail mower that she dragged
across every bit of beauty that sprang unbidden,

cutting it all down like a man

in a poem about reaping written by a man.

THE PAST IN PASTORAL

Winter, the woods are a crowd of bark. Chinaberry, ligustrum, nandina: which matters more, beautiful names or the fact that they're nonnative species? Name aside, nandina is an imperfectly lovely shrub for about two weeks a year, when it pushes out too-little pink or white buds on brushy branches with sharp-tipped red and green leaves. Its berries are poisonous to songbirds. Nonetheless, you can spend time with nandina, even grow to appreciate it. A poet wants beauty—beautiful names, beautiful plants, beautiful scenes—but an environmentally minded poet, who knows that the nandina's roots displace other plants in the surrounding soil, knows that uncomplicated beauty is tough to come by.

Below the skeletal canopy: leaves, stalwart grasses, a boy in black clothing cutting through the woods on his way to work at a restaurant whose name is on his shirt. The Greenbelt, as we call it, is undevelopable land on the floodplain, swamped by the creek every spring and bordered on one side by train tracks riding high on a gravelly embankment. When a freight train passes: a grinding of train cars piled high with car chassis or tawny rocks. The train cars' graffitied sides begin their hypnotism, *follow me, follow me*, but my eyes prefer the trees. Close and quivering in the wind, high in a denuded hackberry, flashes a green sprig that is—small round leaves, thick stems, pearly berries, oh boy—a mistletoe. Underneath, I purse my lips because I love the idea of a plant-powered kiss. Which matters more, love or the fact that mistletoe is parasitic, gorging on the tree it grows on? I eye the greedy tree lover, easiest to see in winter. Mistletoe might be a mirror.

Come live with me and be my love, the Greenbelt sings to me. The line comes from Christopher Marlowe's "The Passionate Shepherd to His Love"—a pastoral poem, as its speaker is a shepherd and its content includes sheep. Wooing, the shepherd imagines dressing his beloved in garments from the pasture: a flower hat, a gown of myrtle leaves and lambswool, and a "belt of straw and Ivy buds, / With Coral clasps and Amber studs." An extractive sartorial fantasy, the outfit pairs coral with straw, wool with leaves. The poem sidesteps the realities of not only ecosystems but also sheep herding: exposure, loneliness, sheep stench, sheep shit. All that *baa*-ing. If someone were to dress me in garments from the Greenbelt, I would wear a nandina gown—tattered crimson leaves, a bit of blight, too-small buds that bloom in April if I time it right—trimmed in fur pulled from the hungriest garbage-eating coyotes, a belt of poison ivy buds with beer tab clasps and pebble studs.

The woods are parkland, by which I mean they are public, but we are not supposed to cross the train tracks, a trespass that circumvents a mile walk to a six-year-old's birthday party. One Saturday, my daughters and I scrambled up the loose rock embankment, stepping over the rails and ties, scrambled down the other side, crossed a dirty puddle, and climbed over the type of metal guardrail that borders highways to end up at the back of an apartment complex. "Whose woods these are I think I know" comes from another pastoral. It's night when Robert Frost's traveler pauses a little too long in the woods he doesn't own, thinking about property, how a woods someone owns can be faithless, abetting intimacies and trespasses. It was also night when my daughters and I left the party, and I used the flashlight on my phone to navigate us across the puddle, over the tracks, and through the woods. Our crossing was cold and quick and then we were back in our neighborhood and walking home for bedtime. At night, the Greenbelt is a sleeping ground of tattered tents, tarps, and tipped-over shopping carts for the sunburned and underfed, who carry their possessions in plastic bags, backpacks, and dingy strollers when they move through the city, through land they do not own.

The pastoral stakes a claim on a place, no matter who owns it, visits it, works in it, lives in it, or sleeps in it. The pastoral craves intimacy but discovers that environments are not promiscuous enough to let them all the way in. *Map your lost fields and meadows*, Gaston Bachelard's *The Poetics of Space* told me. I wrote a note to myself: *Make a map of your lost fields and meadows*, and the note followed me from state to state, occupying a slip of paper or fluttering on a Post-it and finally floating in various Word documents in my computer, where it commanded me to do something I can't. How can I map what never was or will be? I was too busy experiencing what happened in my lost fields or meadows to note their particular fence lines and low muddy places, their hummocks and stones. The pastoral poet enacts an excursion from the city to the countryside, pretending that their lost fields and meadows aren't lost, no, no: the grasses that once echoed their wants can be reassembled. Though the words are etymologically unrelated, is it any wonder that the word *past* is in *pastoral*? The pastoral holds an experience that soothes and shines more in memory than it did in the moment. The past in the pastoral is comfortable (*pastoral* comes from the Latin for *shepherd*, whose job is care), whereas the present is uneasy and the future, frightening. To dig into the etymology of *past* is to find the words *passage* and *passing* and imagine something carrying and carried away, like a train. The pastoral chases the impossible dream of describing a place after the experience of it has passed, yet in truth, both the place and the experience are gone.

One poet follows a rocky road up a hill toward racing clouds. His coat has a ragged hem and its pockets are stretched from holding sticks that he collects from roadsides to feed the fireplace at home in the evening. But now it's daytime. There's a field of spring barley and a young girl alone in it, swinging her scythe and singing a work song that distance makes unintelligible. The wind from the firth musses her yellow hair. "Will no one tell me what she sings?—" the poet asks. He's frustrated, but he must enjoy the frustration, because he doesn't draw close enough to hear her song. If he did, he might see the split on the girl's thumb where the cold has broken down the tissue of her skin, the calluses on her palms, or a sore on her lip. While writing "The Solitary Reaper," if William Wordsworth had gotten close enough to the reaper to hear her song, she wouldn't be solitary anymore. Her words would mix with his. Predicated on distance and impression, the pastoral invited Wordsworth to overwrite the reaper's words and hardship, the contours of the barley field she labored in but in all likelihood didn't own. The poet will never know her field song. He goes home to write his poem by the fire. The only song, a tourist's song, is his.

The field has other voices. In his eerie story "The Sound Machine," Roald Dahl describes a machine through whose headphones a man hears roses screaming when his neighbor cuts them: "A throatless, inhuman shriek, sharp and short, very clear and cold. The note itself possessed a very minor, metallic quality that he had never heard before." He takes an axe to a tree in a nearby park early one morning and, through his headphones there, hears a deep sorrowful moan. The most interesting poetry about the natural world is like that machine in Dahl's story, a machine that lets us listen to all the little voices in the air. This kind of poetry acknowledges an obligation to listen and mourn our lost fields and meadows, our species, weathers, glaciers, and shorelines, gone. Dahl's sound machine is "about three feet long, the shape of a child's coffin." The first time the protagonist takes it out of the shed and onto his close-cropped lawn, it's so heavy that he must hold it with both hands.

Now gone: the field I walked into after the rain, age seven or eight, carrying a rainbow-colored eraser shaped like a clothespin, impossibly small and beautiful and, like a real clothespin, held shut by two metal arms and a small coiled metal spring. The grass swiped at my jeans with a rasping sound and soaked them damp and dark up to my knees. I realized that the eraser was no longer in my hand and was somewhere deep in the mud and grasses that smelled like honey. The field, now gone, where I first saw the flattened dry whorl of a deer's bed in the grass; the fields, now gone, where I ran after a softball and sometimes caught it, and the fields, now gone, where I ran after a soccer ball and sometimes kicked it; the field, now gone, that held a dappled dark-gray pony named Topaz, also gone, to whom I fed circular mints from a blue and green paper-and-foil sleeve, letting his breath create a mist over my palm and inner wrist; the field, now gone, where crop circles appeared overnight, vaguely hieroglyphic patterns of flattened grasses that the farmers said had been made by aliens; the high school soccer field, now gone, where a kisser and I went to kiss at night; the lacrosse field, the football field, the baseball field, the field hockey field: gone, gone, gone, gone. I was even farther afield when I crushed the grasses and was swallowed, but only for a few minutes, by a man who was not my friend. In another time and place, in another meadow that's gone, an herbalist taught me how to harvest purple wildflowers called elephant-head lousewort for a tincture. That was the meadow in which I said yes to someone, and then, later, when that meadow was covered with snow, it was already gone as I pulled my daughters, my hearts, across it in sleds.

DECEMBER

It was never supposed to snow
here, and yet
it was snowing, big flakes tearing down
   over the Edwards Plateau like the sky
         had crumbled. My friend and I drank

   cold wine while our children played
inside with masks
on a big white bed. Another afternoon,
   my daughters sang a song about lords
         and camp that I didn't

   understand, but they didn't like me
to ask what it meant, and
instead of answering rolled down the hill
   in their pajamas. Their
         first secret. Then:

   first bright-red manicure, first
chipped nail, first note taped to the door
saying don't come in. I went
   to the museum instead
         and stared a long time

   at the draft on which Anne Sexton
had scrawled, "At last I found you, you funny
old story-poem!" and felt a happy
   envy, happy for her
         but not for me.

Then: first time on ice skates,
chick-chicking around the rink, a string
of beads draped over one daughter's head
    and my gold necklace still tangled
            by the sink. Snow

    rolled over the prairie and held
the fence shadows when we threw
golden hay to the ponies who lived outside
    all winter. The black-and-white barn cat
            was still alive

    and ate nervously in the garage,
where snow chains glittered on the floor. One night
I told a restaurant it was my husband's birthday
    and they gave us a sundae. It was
            his birthday, and at this point

    we were far from the Edwards Plateau.
I can't remember when we left for that trip but I know
on the last day of December we had to go home
    and in the airport, waiting for the plane, I arranged
    our winter coats so that mine
            was holding everyone else's.

FOUR

MOTHER CARDINAL RHYME

Cheer and cheer and cheer, she sings
a nesting song on nesting wings.
Laurel, sorrel, a quarrel sung
flying into her reflection.
She hates the window,
hits the window
with a violent faith.
Choosing wrong
she sings her song
and a grackle eats her eggs.

MOTHERHOOD

One long-ago summer, what fuss I felt
seemed felt by every gorgeous
prairie part: it bore
the sound of cottonwoods hounded by wind and pooled
like the shade in distant hillside clefts, and the grasses
                crowding the path I walked told me
                        to tell myself
                              that when the field flowered white,
      green, and purple with sego lily, sand lily, and prairie star,
      the field and I were in love.

Who falls in love with a field? A poet. A
child. Persephone, wending
to a far corner. Me, before
I walked into a field at night
with a man I thought was my friend.
                A married man's craving
                        for a woman
                          who isn't his wife is an old
      story, but I still had yet to learn how it would hurt me
      in particular, and therein lay novelty.

You are wondering what all of this has to do with motherhood.

That night in the field, all the eggs basketed inside me
lay down with me when I lay down
next to the man who would not
be the father of my daughters, and all

the eggs turned when I turned
                    from my back to my stomach and bent
            the grasses.
            The summer air,
        the owls, mice, voles, rabbits, spiders, and gnats, the coyotes
        that died under cars on the black road, the dogs

and cats, the lilacs and overhanging trees, and my path
through the grasses: I carry them
like daughters. I carried part
of my daughters through them, and the memory
of the field that night keeps twisting
                    inside me like a virus
                            because my daughters
                    were with us,
        learning how a woman can be loved
        for her choicelessness.

In the days that followed, my daughters
were with us when he touched me
under the hem of my shirt, on my wrist
where my beaded bracelet turned
and clicked, when he wept, spoke of his wife
                and the predicament
                        of his want.
                        What did I want?
        In my diary from that time
        I allowed myself no interiority, no desire

or fear. I spent my heart
naming the grasses—Junegrass, bluegrass, and needle-and-thread—
instead of writing about walking into them. I told myself

I loved the field because it was too shameful
to admit I'd fallen in love with him
                    while he was trying to fuck me.
                                   Do you hear the owls?
                                   asked the note that he slid
          under my bedroom door one night.
The owlets in a nearby nest shrieked

for their mother. I could hear them from my bed.
This was the moment for me in my romantic nightdress
to open the door and finally say yes
let's listen together to the owlets, the wind tossing
cottonwood leaves, and the little foxes who drop mouthfuls
                    of lilies from their teeth to bark
                                   at moths
                                   behind the barn,
          but I was beginning to learn that a world
          with that much beauty could only exist

in my poetry. It was a pretty place
where this man had power over me, and I was beginning to see
that it was ugly. As our friendship declined
into torture, the prairie grew hotter. The sun
beat down onto my forehead
                    like I was a statuette. I still confused passivity
                                   with dignity.
                                   I didn't blame
          the sun: it burned me
          because it was on fire. I didn't blame

the man: he could want me
but not want to leave his wife for me

because he had power.
On a hot afternoon, he and I walked
into the field one last time. Near brushy trees
                    we heard thrashing, breaking branches, and the chuffing
                            of a beast.
                    What makes it hard to say
            that I fell in love with this man, or that he fell in love
            with me, is what happened next:

he shoved me toward the animal we couldn't see and fled
through the saltgrass and blue flax. What we'd heard
was a deer, her pelt velvety with fear, her fawns
somewhere near, and once she pounded away and was gone
it would still take more time for me to see
                    that nobody and nothing in that place,
                            not the man, not
                            the field, not even
            the sunflower and yarrow, would take care of me
            or teach me how to care. It was too beautiful there.

Motherhood would be for me a country
of rage. I live there now,
kicking the shame of what happened to me.
Now I hate the story of how flowers bloom in the girl's footsteps
and a stranger's hand around her waist resembles rapture
                    before the field erases her. What
                            did she want?
                    The story never
            lets us know Persephone, what hopes
            ran through her like glitter

through a stone. This is a poem about motherhood

because now, when I think of the field, I imagine my daughters are there

with a man who uses their passivity to test

his power. It's an old story: he rests his head on one

daughter's shoulder and then on the other daughter's shoulder.

He is about to make them sad

for a long time. Now

that I'm a mother

I understand Demeter, why she walked the earth

and devastated it.

MOTHERS

Mother alkali
Mother Bell
Mother bomb
Mother borough
Mother Bunch
Mother Carey
Mother cat
Mother cell
Mother church
Mother city
Mother clove
Mother coal
Mother colony
Mother complex
Mother country
Mother cow
Mother craft
Mother cult
Mother dialect
Mother Earth
Mother English
Mother General
Mother goddess
Mother heart
Mother hen
Mother house
Mother Hubbard
Mother humper

Mother idea

Mother image

Mother imago

Mother-in-law

Mother instinct

Mother jumper

Mother kingdom

Mother language

Mother liquid

Mother liquor

Mother lode

Mother lodge

Mother love

Mother lye

Mother maid

Mother maiden

Mother mark

Mother metal

Mother Midnight

Mother milk

Mother mind

Mother mold

Mother Nature

Mother of all

Mother of amethyst

Mother of anchovies

Mother of emeralds

Mother of Floods

Mother of God

Mother of gold

Mother of grapes

Mother of millions

Mother of months
Mother of pearl
Mother of States
Mother of the evening
Mother of the herrings
Mother of the maids
Mother of the mine
Mother of the wood
Mother of thousands
Mother of thyme
Mother of wheat
Mother of vinegar
Mother of yaws
Mother pain
Mother pang
Mother pity
Mother plan
Mother plane
Mother plant
Mother Prioress
Mother queen
Mother queller
Mother root
Mother sheep
Mother ship
Mother skein
Mother speech
Mother star
Mother stone
Mother tongue
Mother vein
Mother Vicaress

Mother want
Mother wasp
Mother water
Mother wit
Mother wool
Motherboard
Motherfucker
Motherland

THIRD PERSON

And on the second morning after she left
Hansel and Gretel in the woods, they called
on FaceTime. She asked to see the far-off home
in which they lived. They thrust the small glass screen
around and often dropped it, so the house
lurched and disturbed her stomach. *There's the couch,
the chair*, they said. *The stove and oven knobs.*
Please be careful, she said. *Nibble, nibble,
gnaw*, they sang, showing her via phone
the rough-hewn rafters and, for a dark pause,
the carpet fibers. *Rain*, they said, and thrust
the phone eye to the drops that spilled off the roof
and through the pines but which the phone could not
let her see. *I wish I could see the rain*,
she said to her flushed-faced children, who
were wearing pajamas far too warm for spring.
Are you two hot? she asked. *Nibble, nibble,
gnaw*, they sang, showing her two hard nests
they'd built of blocks for the toy birds that warbled
when squashed. *Have you had breakfast yet?* she asked.
The children thought she meant the birds. *Fat worms!*
they said, and accidently pressed Mute.
A pantomime of care progressed around
the wooden nests in the house where, until
two days ago, she'd lived with them. *I'll be
home soon*, she said as the children threw
foam packing peanuts at the birds. Who'd clean
the crumbs the birds would never nibble? Who

would feed her fire-cheeked children? Eventually
the sound came back to their story, which wasn't one
she thought she knew. The witch and mother now
seemed fungible, a wooden home no safer
than a cake one. *What else, Mama?* they asked,
clamoring big-faced on the cramping screen.
Since she had nothing else, she watched her children
grunt and scratch and bite each other, fighting
over who would push the red button
to end the call and make her disappear.

PEDERNALES FALLS

The water's distress as it descends over rocks is what makes
a rapid, rapid as in a pace too fast to follow or a place
where she swam and was happiest that year, in a river
she threw herself into like a coin, wishing upon herself
to forget how hot the day, hard the spring, and who she was,
wishing to be forgotten by every part of her life that wasn't
water, wearing the current's wavelets like the silk dress
she lost somewhere between her daughters' ankle wens
from poison ivy and fairy houses built of moss, and when one daughter
said later, when they were home and she'd been remembered,
I still feel the rapids, the daughter fluttered her legs to show the shape
of what was gone, was ghost, and all her coins weighed down
the pink ceramic pig that watched the mother say she felt the rapids too,
when really she'd wished too well, no longer did she feel
the water, and this was loss, distress, a dress she didn't remember
the feel of, maybe never felt, even when she had the chance.

PANDEMIC PARABLE

I'll check on the flowers, the mother says to no one as she leaves the house.

Dregs of yesterday's water silver the bottom of the backyard inflatable pool.

By flowers she doesn't mean mistflower bounced over by monarchs, not calico lantana.

Out the back gate, she skulks through alleys instead of streets.

Not indigo dayflower, not the particulate white hedge parsley in the alley bracken.

A fabulously tailed red fox trots in the distance, delivering her trouble to the morning as if she owned it.

One morning, the mother's daughters owned a roly-poly.

Pill bug, doodle bug, wood shrimp: going by many names seems a freedom.

When she believed she was free to choose the kind of mother she would be, the mother chose a name from a list: Mama, Mommy, Ma, Mom, Mum, Mummy, etc.

Conglobation is the name for curling up into a tiny blue-black ball in a child's palm.

Her daughters made a house using the biggest American beautyberry leaf they'd ever seen, an asphalt chunk, and a petal from the neighbor's knockout rose.

Is your roly-poly still living there? is a question she knows better than to ask her daughters.

Her daughters are still so young that they've cried almost every day they've been alive.

The mother cries herself that spring, though crying doesn't make her feel like a girl.

Each footfall presses her sadness into the alley dirt and rock.

Jane Eyre: "It is not without a certain wild pleasure that I run before the wind."

Whither pleasure? is a question the mother knows better than to ask herself that spring.

She knows the fox has found pleasure when the neighbor's peacocks start crying, *Maw! Maw!*

Licking the knife, forgoing sunscreen, throwing out her daughters' rumpled drawings: the mother's pleasures feel most wrong when executed in secret.

A child never thinks, *I'm supposed to do X, but I want to do Y.*

A child rips the silky pink petals off the neighbor's knockout rose.

The scent of confederate jasmine overtakes the air.

Confederate is the name for someone or something united in a league, alliance, or confederacy.

The name makes her wary of the flowers.

Hers is a country with an unshakeable history.

We've been waiting for you, say the flowers to no one.

Like the datura, lantana, and morning glory, the confederate jasmine is toxic if eaten.

To what extent has she already been poisoned?

Out creeps the evergreen want: to disappear for a bit, not come when called.

Mr. Rolls is what they called the roly-poly when they wanted it to come to them.

It rolled in a ball and did not come.

To explain the pleasure the mother takes in disappearing from her home requires her to explain the danger she feels when it's the only thing she wants.

Her daughters collect the bright red seeds of the Texas mountain laurel and leave them all over the house.

They know the seeds are poisonous but don't know their names.

Her daughters know that people are dying that spring but don't know their names. If she runs away from home, how will the mother teach them not to run away?

Maybe the mother is wrong, and they are teaching her to stay.

Jostling paints and glitter, they upset the face painter at the birthday party years ago.

Holding a delicate brush, the face painter asked her daughter what she wanted on her face, and her daughter said, *My face*.

BURNING CREEK

The creek bed without water made the mother
suggestible. The cleft left

by histories of water now held rank grass, rocks
and snaked through oaks. She

made a note to conjure the creek bed when she next
swore allegiance to the imagination,

the thinking that thinks this bed once
held water that gave

its sound to the grove, a trickle
then a roar like the fire the creek was named

for. Which image of motherhood would she choose?
Motherhood as water

or bed, motherhood as the event or the shape
it left? Not a golden-cheeked

warbler, not a cardinal, not an undulant
shade, the answer she looked for in the creek bed

wasn't there, and it was the never finding
that she was a little bit in love with,

because it tethered her to grass and rocks

and to the prairie coneflower, prickly poppy, and desert

chicory wobbled over by wind.
                              The next day came walls

of rain and the creek, she knew, would fill
with water that dragged the long stalks of grass

under. But by then she was gone
from the grove where she could have seen the creek

split itself around rocks and send frail twigs spinning
downstream. Instead, she was home

where there was a children's table and children asking
for blue, and from the bucket

of crayons and markers, she had to choose:
violet-blue, blue-violet, blue marble, sky,

blue moon, midnight, maximum blue, little boy blue,
bluebonnet, cornflower, celestial

blue, blue bell, periwinkle, indigo, larkspur,
wild blue yonder, robin's egg, cobalt

blue, green-blue, blue-green, teal, mermaid tail...

FIVE

FRONT YARD RHYME

Stone path, oat grass, stray cat, snare,
feather drift in feather air.
Laurel, anthill, train horn blare,
pecan shell shards on the stair.
One cat gnaws,
one wing tears.
One less song for the power line to bear.
Coo-OO-oo, she sang, my dear.

NEIGHBORING

This afternoon I believe the shadows.
In the November hour before the hour
when windows blacken,
the shadows place their faith in our kitchen
rather than the weeping persimmon tree
or the train tracks in the gorge
behind the house. The backsplash
and knife block, it seems, have been waiting
for them: the cold tiles flicker as if lit
and the wooden knife handles show more edge
than I'm used to holding in my hand.
Soon I'll chop garlic for soup. Soon
the rats will come to nestle and curl in the nest
they've built in our attic. There was a pang
I used to feel when I thought of nests
but I know now that I wasn't thinking of the nests
of rats, or how, if I followed an overgrown trail
down to the train tracks, pushing through mistflower
and beautyberry and crossing a dry creek, I would arrive
at a filthy blue tarp strung between brambles
that was obviously someone's home and turn
and run. Of my neighbors in this new place, I know
the stone in the leaf pile, a stump
crawling with ants beside the back gate
and a neighbor girl almost tall enough to climb
our fence. I've asked no one to come to dinner
though each night the rats arrive
at dinnertime and scratch at the ceiling
with the insistence of providence.

COLLECTED TYPOS

Each morning, the sun
came through the snow-piled pines
                            to shovel up

the night. This was New Hampshire.
A New Hampshire of the mind, a New
                            Hampshire of mine

where I lived for wind.
For a winter. Where I wrote an essay, four lines
                            of a poem, and missed

my stapler. *Why stapler?* the close
reader asks. My answer: my friend Tom
                            gave me the word

in a mist. In a list. Of typos.
I hope I didn't miss you, he wrote on the list
                            of typos. Hope

for accuracy hovers like a bird
of prey over my memory of that hibernal era. That
                            errata. He didn't miss

me: I have the list he gave me
in New Hampshire before we both
                            left, before the month

was other. Was over. When I think over
that winter in New Hampshire, I remember
                    a small fireplace's worth

of fire. *Safe home!* he wrote on the list, and *Love*.
When I wrote in New Hampshire my writing hand
                    obstructed my light,

shadowing the page like a flock
of nights. A flock of eights. Qué bonitos
                    ochos tienes! Why

should eyes be lovely anyway. What lovely
eyes you have, said nobody, especially
                    not Tom, to me

in New Hampshire. *Que te vaya bien!*
means good luck, which is close
                    to *Safe home!*

an expression I learned from Tom, who lost
his home soon after New Hampshire, and lived
                    thenceforth under roofs

that were not his own. Not his home.
No fixed above. No fixed abode.
                    Why should luck

have landed me here, years later, in a safe home
with light to write by and opals
                    on a silk cord

around my neck. Opals make a person
emotional, I'm told, though to me
                    they're capsules of snow

and the number of days in a row
I spent in New Hampshire a long
                    time ago. I take

the opals off when I feel my sadness
well. My sadness swell. My sadness swells
                    tonight, in my home,

where I night. Where I write. Tonight is not
new, not New Hampshire blurred
                    by winter, not warmed

by whiskey that Tom poured in the opal
firelight. Light is a mood, though *relámpago*
                    is what I think,

my mind's lightning flashing me back
to a long-ago winter and the patter
                    of spent snow shucked off

the pangs. The pines. I met Tom before
I knew I would die, and now he's dead.
                    He was my friend

for one winter, a lightning-bright
scar. Spar. Star. This should align with
                    the following line,

my list of typos tells me. The list
that Tom gave me. *Well*
                    I wished you had been

at Keene last night, Tom wrote,
when after an eight-hour bus trip
                    I had to wait

forty minutes for a taxi. In truth he wrote *our*
bus trip. I corrected it. Am I wrong
                    to confuse friendship

with time. Both I share, both I spend, both
I waste. I shared and spent
                    one winter with Tom,

one road winding through pangs, one field,
one wind through the waste.
                    What remains are

the errata, the mistaking
I make in order
                    to keep making.

WHAT IF THE LUMINOUS

The Cave Without a Name, a National Natural Landmark in the
Texas Hill Country, was discovered by siblings James, Harold, and
Mary McGrath in the 1930s when they were out looking for lost
sheep. The cave entrance was marked by a sinkhole and the remains
of an old moonshiner's still. It was said that, because Mary was the
smallest, her brothers lowered her down into the cave with a rope.

What lights up a morning
is juice in the low glasses, egg yolks
in the yellow cake, a feather in the dust

out the back door, sun on the knots
of the barbed-wire fence, bells on the sheep's necks
nodding away into the brush, and a grass blade

twitched by a furred life lived mostly invisibly
near the ground. The ground gives off its groundshine
that the children are low enough to see.

What lights up a night is the moon
and what lights up the bright part of the moon is the sun
that the house spins away from every evening

carrying the children's sleeping bodies
and the blackened windows with it.
What lights up the dark part of the moon

to make a grayish glow beside the bright
is earthshine reflecting off the elsewhere lakes and snow
drifting in the children's minds.

What lights up a hallway is borrowed light
that falls through the kitchen window or through
the pane of square glass set in the back door,

and to walk one night through the borrowed light and out
the door is to go darkly away, swinging
a lantern, running on feet familiar with the path

so that it doesn't matter whether the eyes
can see it or not, because the children are never more alive
than when they walk through the field

that the sheep hide themselves inside, the field
that the moonshine runs over, the cedars and creek
gone a weird white. Had the children been born earlier,

before pasture, before sheep, before the moths
striking softly against them, they would have come across
a low fire under a still and someone cooking water, sugar,

yeast, and corn into moonshine.
When the sheep disappear, the children know
where in the pasture to find them but not the sinkhole

they'll find there. If the goal of pruning a tree
is to make spaces a bird could fly through, perhaps the goal
of water is to make fissures in the limestone to fall through

below the corroded still the sheep like to sleep
with silenced bells next to, and perhaps the goal
of the rope is to drop through the hole

so the girl can lower herself into the cave.
What if the luminous has never been
the low fire, the lantern, not the moonshine on pasture, not

a burning drink and what it ignites in the mind. What
if the luminous has never been the juice, the cake, the feather's
iridescence, the sharp fence, or the hidden sheep.

I was never afraid, says the woman
who the girl sliding down a scratchy rope
grows up to be. The cave she lowers herself into

shines like nothing she knows and she knows
not to be afraid of the water running over the rock,
the watershine where the rock gleams out of the dark

and the cave makes itself divine for her.
She feels thirst and the thirst for the cave
to show her how it began. When she places her palm

against what shines, she remembers looking
into a lost lamb's eyes and knowing nothing about what it saw
except that it was magnificent and private.

ON FIRST LOOKING INTO EMILY WILSON'S HOMER

Each summer I swim in a lake that the sun turns gold
toward sister islands piled high with pines
as if I were a homegoing heroine
whom gods had spelled from becoming ugly or old.
Water-going women are not, I've been told,
as epically interesting as goddesses, monsters, or sirens;
yet after Homer's princess washes garments,
she saves a hero who Wilson never describes as bold.
Knowing this is like reaching the distant rise
of a new shore, having swum faster than
a wooden boat helmed by a war-wise
king, but it's the moment when
Penelope says, "I am the prize,"
that I continue to take most pleasure in.

TANGERINE CROSSVINE

I try to clean up the ecstatic vines.
Gardeners have a kink for obedience.

Gardeners have a kink for obedience
like each twist of a backyard chain link fence.

Like each twist of a backyard chain link fence
I'm only made of pieces in a pattern.

Only made of pieces in a pattern
I try to keep up with the ecstatic vines.

THE SEEDS

The mouth closes around a word full of O.
Hope: a plea, a sigh, a piece
of enclosed land, a small bounded valley. Also an inlet, a small bay, a haven
in the lake I steer my boat into

                    (dropping my good shoes
                    and then my feet into the biting
                    water) because the water
reminds me of a dance floor. O,

                          I'm thirty-four again, in summer,
                          giddied by grease smoke and soft serve

from the fast food shacks, my blown-back hair
mimicking the bankside cattails
each time I do a double take
at the drive-in marquee. Each time
I ride a car around the lake

it's an odyssey.
                Did I hope
                      like Odysseus or like Penelope?
                I no longer remember the steps

the stranger and I danced
at the party by the water, expecting
what we desired. Sweat darkened my dove-gray
dress, nasturtium petals toppled
through the salad leaves, wavelets
from a storm far offshore

met the black breakwater and surged

upward. Like the particular hop
in the stomach when I see pews
with sky blue cushions stacked
in the back of a pickup truck on the highway, or

when we pushed our beds together
in the damp rented room. The lake had already
rolled in our sheets, mildew
marbled the walls with fungal mist.

I hoped the storm would stay offshore.
I hoped a storm would come in.

There's a hope chest at the foot of the bed
that a girl should pack with a heart-shaped
stone, a nightgown, and a clump
of forget-me-nots she finds by the stream.
Not me. I packed
a jar of lake water
and my grandmother's two sets of silver
whose tarnishes clouded the spoons
darker, reminding me to be diligent,
for no woman
has swallowed a storm. Along
with Faith and Love, Hope
is personified as one of the three
heavenly female graces.

Emily Dickinson: "'Hope' is a thing with feathers."
Gertrude Stein: "I hope, I hope and I hope. I hope that I hope and I hope."

Dorothy Wordsworth: "I lingered out of doors in hope of hearing my Brothers
  tread."

Is hope the province of women?

        As I hope to show: a means
    of arguing gently
in a scholarly essay. The blind peer reviewer
chastised me for using it, correctly assuming
my gender. The water rings on my wooden desk
                marked pools
            of thought that I dared
to reign.
        Delete, delete. I erased hope
in order to argue, I presumed,
like a man, offering an analysis
as the only route
to the palace.
        "I hope all will be well," Ophelia says, but we know
she is doomed when she starts talking
about fennel, columbines, violets, and rue.

                Not a hope in hell, hope against hope, hope
                for the best.

Ophelia reminds me
        of the mountain laurel
the botanical illustrator placed in a bathtub full of water
to paint branch and bloom undistorted
by gravity, lifelike even
as they died. I've heard
        of a horticulturalist who entered a field

thinking that whatever he needed

he would find, a method I find irresistible

until I suspect it is only available

to men. The difference between hope

      and entitlement is the difference

            between imagining how much hay

            the meadow will bear

                and assuming your winter ponies

                won't starve.

Gertrude Stein again: "Hope in gates, hope in spoons, hope in doors, hope in
    tables, no hope in daintiness and determination. Hope in dates."

Historical hope: on the Internet

you can find a poster of the man who became

president. Red and blue, the word in all caps

like a vine twisting up the stake

of history. A long

time ago. Meanwhile,

I circumnavigated a minor lake.

In a car. I was thirty-four

              when I put down the Ziploc of candy

              I'd been surviving on and admitted

              that I was a woman. I stopped hoping

to be a flower girl in a wedding

wearing a daisy crown and scattering petals

from a demolished rose.

           Flower girls first

           appeared in weddings

in ancient Rome, carrying bundles

             of wheat. Hope in the body, fertility

in the field. I can say

that I hoped to be the symbol

of fertility, hoped to promise

the betrothed a green everlasting earth

as they stepped

into history, but I never knew

who the bride and groom

would be. I think what I really hoped for

is what I miss hoping for:

to be a wild queen, married

to the flowers and sailing

through a field

where fishes swim in the dew.

I was a child

until I was thirty-four

and met the love I'd hoped for. If I hadn't hoped

to be a wild queen, I may not have hoped for a field,

a small bounded valley

for my dream daughters

to drift into

like two seeds.

How long until winter? Will

the shaggy ponies starve? my real daughters ask me now.

Their questions are the same as mine

in that they have no answers,

though the lessons of damage

are everywhere. As in the parable

of the Texas mountain laurel, whose bright red seeds

I unwrapped one afternoon

from a seed pod to place

in my daughters' hands. The girls were young

and tried, by resting

the seeds on branches,

to put them back

in the tree.

That it was too late

to undo

what I'd done

to the tree

wasn't what I'd hoped to show, though

it was a better lesson, reminding me that only Penelope

can undo the weaving

on the burial shroud.

I hoped like Penelope until I became

a mother. Now I think of hope

as a swing chained to a branch.

It can be used until

the branch sweeps the ground

with a *shush, shush* because

it cannot bear

so much weight and still loft through

the dream-trafficked air.

I don't care what you say.

A swing may be a child's thing

but the chains

that bind it to the tree

are not.

BLUEBONNET INTERLUDE

How could
we flower
we wonder
in smooth
lawns where
to ask
is to
yield to
a coil
of prairie
one bloom
in size
thriving in
grass blades
by accident
of wind,
drought, grackle-
or mourning-dove-
claw, or—
as remnant
faith would
please to
have us
believe—to
suffuse our
failure to
garden with
blue.

HACKBERRY

A place I love is about to disappear.
When the summer sunset drives
into the west side
               of our house, burning
                         with a heat we've been warned about,

         I look out the two square windows
that are filled with hackberry leaves whose greens
vary according to light and wind
         and whose shade composes a sort-of room
                   for us, under the tree.

               It's said that those who sleep under a hackberry
will be protected from evil spirits,
and I can't stop thinking of how the four of us for years
         blithely slept the sleep of the protected, as if
                   there were no other sleep, and how

               in the daytime, the tree arranged its shade
to let hearts of sunlight fall
on the stone path underneath it. How a scar
         on the tree's bark looked like a brown moth
                   pressed unendingly against it.

               For months all I've wanted is the blessing
of an open window. Maybe also
I've wanted to sleep through the night.
         Tonight is the last night we'll sleep

under the hackberry whose leaves

at sunset cause the walls
and floor to shimmer—
it reminds me of crying.

You can see the tree from the whole house, June says.
When I was younger and walked barefoot on the sharp stones,
Calla says, *I stepped on its roots because they were smooth.*

Kretzschmaria deusta, a beautifully named fungus
ate the roots from the inside

and now what held my daughter's weight
are columns of nothing. Now
the tips of the live oaks softly brush
the tips of the hackberry canopy.
I would like to believe in tenderness.

Earlier today, I tried my arms
around the tree
but they wouldn't wrap all the way
around and, actually, the tree scratched
my skin, and tomorrow

a crew will cut it down.
Some people call a hackberry
a junk tree or trash tree,
throwing shade. I love the tree's shade, and now
it will be gone,

as will the sunlight in the shape

of love, and the evil spirits

will do as they please with our nights.

How do I write this poem, I ask my family

as we sit together in the disappearing room.

NOTES

"Sunday" was written after reading Brigit Pegeen Kelly's poem "Doing Laundry on Sunday," which begins: "So this is the Sabbath" and includes the phrase "as I wait."

"Amistad Gambusia" refers to Alex E. Peden's scholarly paper "Virtual Extinction of *Gambusia amistadensis* n. sp., a Poeciliid Fish from Texas" (*Copeia,* May 22, 1973, Vol. 1973, No. 2, pp. 201-221). Peden writes: "The newly constructed (1968) Amistad Reservoir on the Rio Grande has inundated the Goodenough Spring with more than 30 meters of water. Although some individuals from this population survive in artificial ponds and aquaria, the indigenous stock of *G. amistadensis* is presumably extinct." A subsequent paper, by Clark Hubbs and Buddy Lee Jensen, "Extinction of Gambusia amistadensis, an Endangered Fish" (*Copeia*, Vol, 1984, No. 2 (May 1, 1984), pp. 529-530) follows up on Peden's findings: "He [Peden] further pointed out that survivors of that population survived in artificial pools. Herein we report the extinction of their descendants."

"The Bats": Some language and phrasing in this poem come from Diane Ackerman's "The Bats" (*The New Yorker*, February 21, 1988), which is in part a profile of Merlin D. Tuttle, a bat expert and founder of Bat Conservation International, headquartered in Austin, TX. I also consulted Emily Dickinson's "[The Bat is dun with wrinkled wings]" in which she describes a bat as a "small umbrella, quaintly halved[.]"

"Motherhood" owes its ending to the interpretation of *The Homeric Hymn to Demeter* in Anne Carson's *The Beauty of the Husband*, in which Demeter "walks the world and damages every living thing."

"Burning Creek": The Crayola color chart includes nineteen shades of blue: some of their names, as well as the names of colors in the Crayola blue hue family, appear at the end of this poem.

"Collected Typos" is dedicated to the poet Tom Raworth (1938-2017).

"On First Looking into Emily Wilson's Homer" is for Sari Edelstein.

"The Seeds": The phrase "I don't care what you say" comes from Patrick Rosal's poem "Crew Love Elegy."

ACKNOWLEDGMENTS

I am grateful to the editors and staff of the following publications in which these poems first appeared, often in earlier versions: *A Public Space, Alaska Quarterly Review, Bennington Review, Conjunctions, Ecotone, Feminist Formations, Harvard Review, High Country News, Mississippi Review, Narrative, The Nation, New England Review, New Republic, The New Yorker, Orion, Poem-a-Day, Poetry Northwest, The Rumpus, Sierra, Terrain.org, Tin House, Under a Warm Green Linden, The Yale Review.*

Thank you, also, to Rosa Alcalá for selecting "The Rio Grande" for the 2019 Lucille Medwick Memorial Award, sponsored by the Poetry Society of America. The poem first appeared on the Poetry Society of America website.

I also owe thanks to the editors who included my work in anthologies and other projects. Paisley Rekdal selected "The Seeds" for *The Best American Poetry 2020*, Tracy K. Smith selected "December" for *The Slowdown* and *The Best American Poetry 2021*, and Matthew Zapruder selected "Pandemic Parable" for *The Best American Poetry 2022*. Jenna Clark Embrey included "Girlhood" in *The Gardens of Anuncia* issue of *Lincoln Center Theater Review*. Jenny Browne included "Texas Natives" in the anthology *Texas: Being*; Ann Fisher-Wirth and Laura-Gray Street included "Girlhood" in *Attached to the Living World: A New Ecopoetry Anthology;* Sally Keith included "Girlhood" in an Ecopoetry Now feature at *Poetry Daily*; and Ada Limón included "Hackberry" in *You Are Here: Poetry in the Natural World*.

Thank you to Stuart Hyatt for inviting me to contribute to three different Field Works albums during the time I worked on this book. "What if the Luminous" first appeared as part of the Glen Rose Formation exhibit at Texas State Galleries and on the Field Works album *Glen Rose Formation*; "The Bats" and "Deciduous" first appeared on the Field Works albums *Ultrasonic* and *Maples, Ash, and Oaks: Cedar Instrumentals*, respectively. Thank you to Jennifer Calkins for the invitation to learn about/from the Amistad gambusia and to contribute "Amistad Gambusia" to the Delisted Project—and to Adam Cohen and Bob Edwards for welcoming me into the Ichthyology Collections at the University of Texas while I wrote that poem. These opportunities to spend time with specific places and species always came when I most needed them.

I am grateful for fellowships from Hewnoaks, Marble House Project, and MacDowell: each provided invaluable time, space, and community as I worked on these poems. I am also grateful for the support of Texas State University and my wonderful colleagues there.

Jenny Stephens, Carey Salerno, and the staff of Alice James Books: thank you for taking care of *The Seeds*. Thank you to the friends who read earlier versions of this manuscript and helped me figure out what it could be: Karen Leona Anderson, Jennifer Chang, Leigh Anne Couch, Jenny Kronovet, and Nida Sophasarun. Thank you to the friends who make the writing life less lonely: Sonja Danburg, Carrie Doyle, Sari Edelstein, Farnoosh Fathi, Laura Feldman, Kay Lee Fordham, Louisa Hall, Leila Kempner, Rowena Kennedy-Epstein, Joanna Klink, Cathy Matusow, Jimmy McWilliams, Debra Monroe, Karen Olsson, Lisa Olstein, Maggie Savage, Josie Gill Schlather, Leah Shlachter, Tyler Smith, Lisa Russ Spaar, Mary Helen Specht, Kevin Wilson, and Rachael Wren. To my parents: thank you for your love, which includes giving me my first backyard. Thank you to my brothers for always knowing how to make me laugh. Countless I love yous to Nick, Calla, and June: you help me grow.

RECENT TITLES FROM ALICE JAMES BOOKS

Alice James Books is committed to publishing books that matter. The press was founded in 1973 in Boston, Massachusetts to give women access to publishing. As a cooperative, authors performed the day-to-day undertakings of the press. The press continues to expand and grow from its formative roots, guided by its founding values of access, excellence, inclusivity, and collaboration in publishing. Its mission is to publish books that matter and preserve a place of belonging for poets who inspire us. AJB seeks to broaden our collective interpretation of what constitutes the American poetic voice and is dedicated to helping its artists achieve purposeful engagement with broad audiences and communities nationwide. The press was named for Alice James, sister to William and Henry, whose extraordinary gift for writing went unrecognized during her lifetime.

Designed by Zoe Norvell

Printed by Versa Press